Where Did It Go?

World Book, Inc.
180 North LaSalle Street
Suite 900
Chicago, Illinois 60601
USA

For information about other World Book publications, visit our website at **www.worldbook.com** or call **1-800-WORLDBK (967-5325)**.

Library of Congress Cataloging-in-Publication data has been applied for.
Title: Ugh! Yuck! and Whoa! Where Did It Go?
ISBN: 978-0-7166-3714-1

Ugh! Yuck! and Whoa!
ISBN: 978-0-7166-3708-0 (set, hc)

Also available as:
ISBN: 978-0-7166-3722-6 (e-book)

STAFF

Executive Committee

President
Jim O'Rourke

Vice President and Editor in Chief
Paul A. Kobasa

Vice President, Finance
Donald D. Keller

Vice President, Marketing
Jean Lin

Vice President, International
Maksim Rutenberg

Vice President, Technology
Jason Dole

Director, Human Resources
Bev Ecker

Editorial

Director, Print Publishing
Tom Evans

Writer
Grace Guibert

Editor
Will Adams

Manager, Contracts & Compliance (Rights & Permissions)
Loranne K. Shields

Manager, Indexing Services
David Pofelski

Librarian
S. Thomas Richardson

Digital

Director, Digital Product Development
Erika Meller

Digital Product Manager
Jonathan Wills

Manufacturing/ Production

Manufacturing Manager
Anne Fritzinger

Proofreader
Nathalie Strassheim

Graphics and Design

Senior Art Director
Tom Evans

Senior Designer
Don Di Sante

Media Editor
Rosalia Bledsoe

Special thanks to:

Nature Picture Library

Introduction

Nature is filled with some amazing creatures. From ocean bottoms to mountain tops, from hot deserts to freezing tundra, the *Ugh! Yuck! and Whoa!* books highlight the most extreme animals: the grossest, the deadliest, the strangest, and the ugliest! This book is all about animals that use **camouflage** *(KAM uh flahzh).* **Camouflage** is an animal's color or shape that helps it blend in with its **habitat.** Some animals **mimic** the shape and color of plants or other animals. **Camouflage** and **mimicry** can help animals stay safe from **predators** or surprise their **prey.** Read on to see and learn about the craziest **camouflaged** animals! They come in beautiful colors, take on strange shapes, and can be nearly impossible to spot. This Camo Cover meter will show the strength of each animal's **camouflage.**

LEAF-TAILED GECKO

CAMO COVER
HIGH

Geckos are a type of small lizard that live in warm places. This leaf-tailed gecko blends into the bark and leaves of the trees it climbs. It has a long, flat body and a leaf-shaped tail! The color and patterns of its skin make it almost impossible to spot. Can you find it?

Yuck!

Leaf-tailed geckos don't have eyelids. They keep their eyes clear by licking them! Eeeuuuwww!

ORCHID MANTIS

Mantises are a kind of bug. All kinds of mantises use **camouflage** to blend into their **habitat.** The orchid mantis might be the most beautiful. The orchid mantis lives on flowers called orchids—and it looks just like one! **Camouflage** helps mantises surprise their **prey.**

CAMO COVER

MEDIUM

Other mantises look like plants, too!

Critters that Change Colors

Some animals are experts in **camouflage**. They can change from one color to another to match their surroundings!

Squid

Cuttlefish

Chameleon

Goldenrod crab spider

WILD GROUSE

This little white bird lives in snowy areas of Europe and North America. Its white feathers help it blend into the fluffy snow. Can you spot the bird among the snow and branches?

CAMO COVER
MEDIUM

LEAF-NOSED TWIG SNAKE

This snake is long and skinny. Its coloring helps it blend into trees and vines in the forests where it lives. If the leaf-nosed twig snake stays very still, its **prey** won't even notice that it's there. To hunt, the snake just has to wait for its food to come close. Then, it grabs its lunch!

Whoa!

Male and female leaf-nosed twig snakes look different. Females look a lot like twigs. Males, like the one below, look more like leaves!

PERINGUEY'S ADDER

This snake slithers through the desert sands of the southwestern African country of Namibia *(nuh MIHB ee uh).* The sharp scales that cover its body match the yellow and brown sand. When it hunts, this desert adder sinks into the sand so it's almost invisible to its **prey.**

CAMO COVER
HIGH

MIMIC OCTOPUS

This octopus is named for its ability to **mimic** the shapes of other sea creatures! To scare off animals that might harm it, the **mimic** octopus pretends to be other dangerous animals. It might take the shape of a lionfish—which has poisonous spines—or a sea snake—which has a venomous bite. The **mimic** octopus can pretend to be more than 10 different animals!

CAMO COVER HIGH

To imitate a sea snake, the **mimic** octopus hides in the sand. It extends two of its tentacles to turn itself into a long snake!

LEAFY SEADRAGON

This fish looks like seaweed floating in the ocean. The leafy seadragon has parts that look just like leaves. It blends in perfectly with the kelp, seaweed, and other ocean plants it lives around.

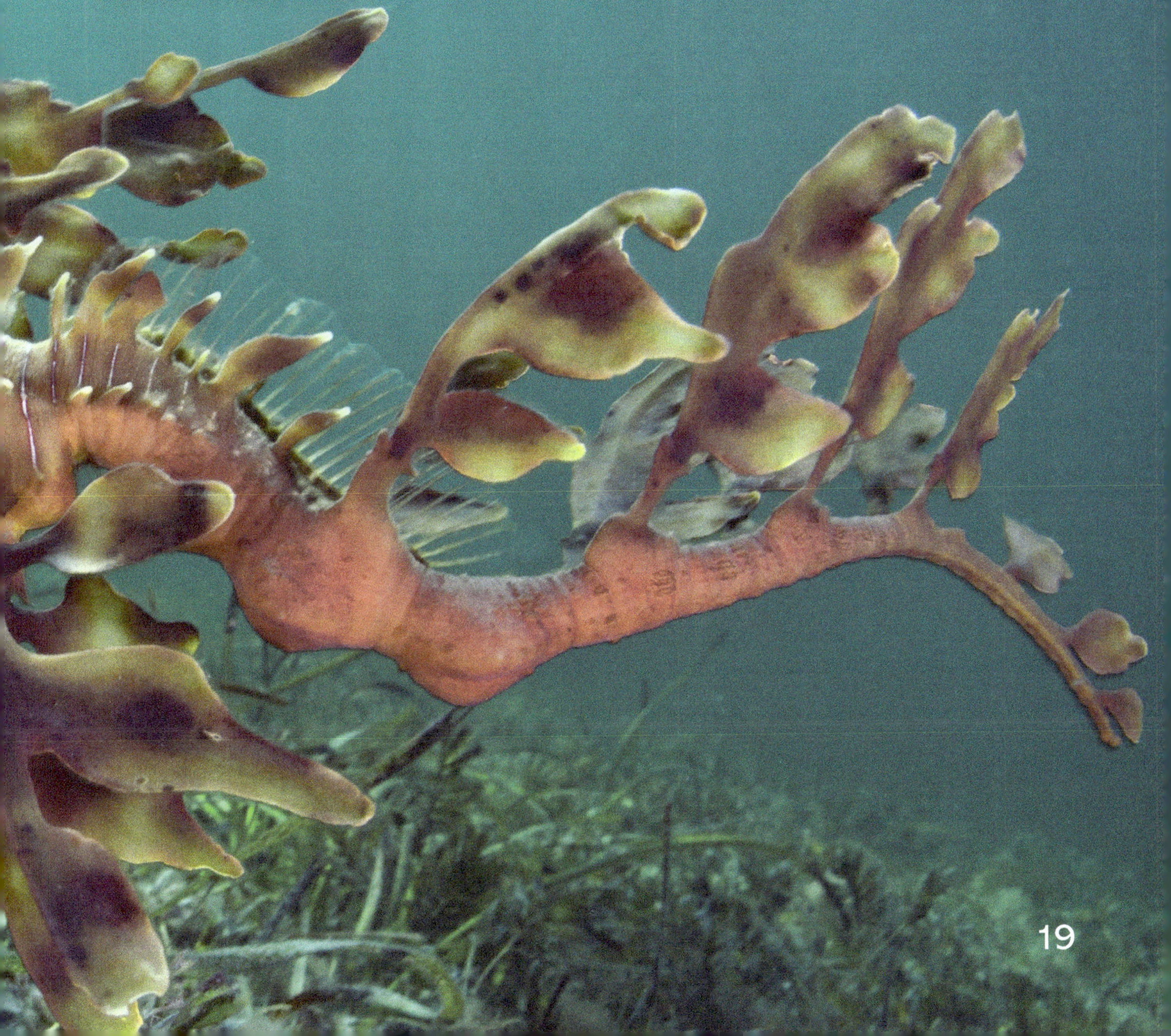

SNOWY OWL
Whoa!
Snowy owls have big yellow eyes.

The snowy owl's wintry white feathers help it blend into the snow! Sometimes, snowy owls have brown markings that match the trees and bushes in the forests where the owls live.

CAMO COVER

MEDIUM

FLOUNDER

Ugh!

Flounders are funky-looking, flat fish. Here is what flounders look like from above!

Flounders live on the bottom of the ocean. One side of their bodies stays pressed against the ocean floor. Both eyes of a flounder are on the top side of its body. Some flounders can even change colors to match the rocks, sand, and plants of the ocean floor.

CAMO COVER
HIGH

THE BIRD-POO SPIDER

This spider looks—and smells—like dried-up bird poo! It can sit on leaves to wait for its **prey,** like flies, to come right up to it. It keeps **predators** away with its gross smell and looks. This spider's fancy name is *Celaenia excavata*. But bird-poo (or bird-droppings) spider is more fun!

CAMO COVER
HIGH

CATERPILLARS

Caterpillars turn into beautiful moths and butterflies. But they have to steer clear of **predators** to do so! Lots of caterpillars are great at blending in to their **habitat.** Some pretend to be more dangerous animals, like spiders or snakes. Some caterpillars even look like poo to keep **predators** away! Yuck!

Brussels lace moth caterpillar

Noctuid moth caterpillar

Swallowtail butterfly caterpillar

Peppered moth caterpillar

ARCTIC FOX

When the snow melts, the Arctic fox sheds some of its white fur. Its darker summer fur helps it blend into the earth and rocks where it lives during warmer months.

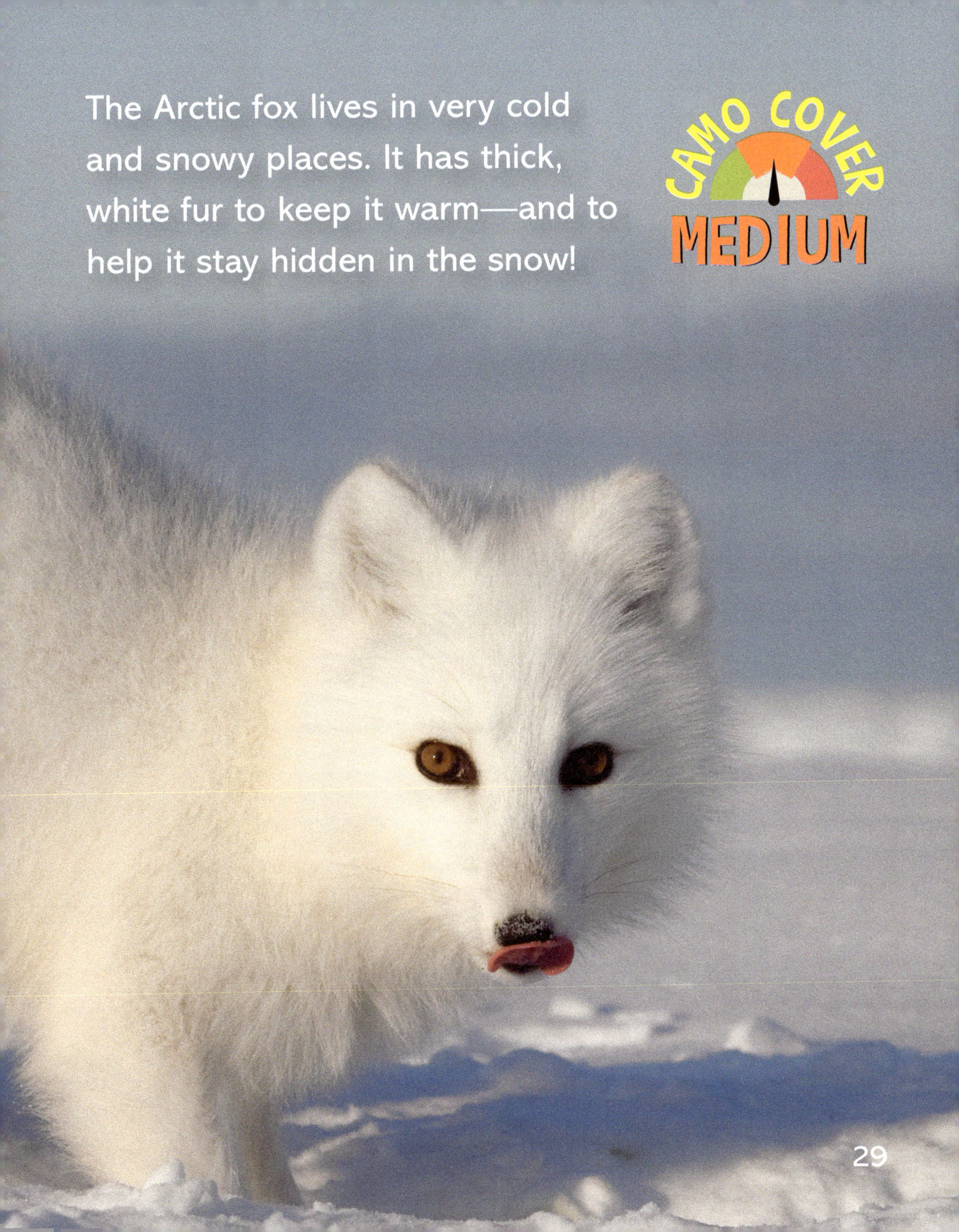

The Arctic fox lives in very cold and snowy places. It has thick, white fur to keep it warm—and to help it stay hidden in the snow!

PYGMY SEAHORSE

These little seahorses live among corals. Corals are rocky **habitats** made by tiny ocean animals called coral **polyps** *(PAHL ihps)*. Corals are home to lots of life. Pygmy seahorses blend right in! They are no bigger than a few grains of rice.

CAMO COVER
MEDIUM

TIGER

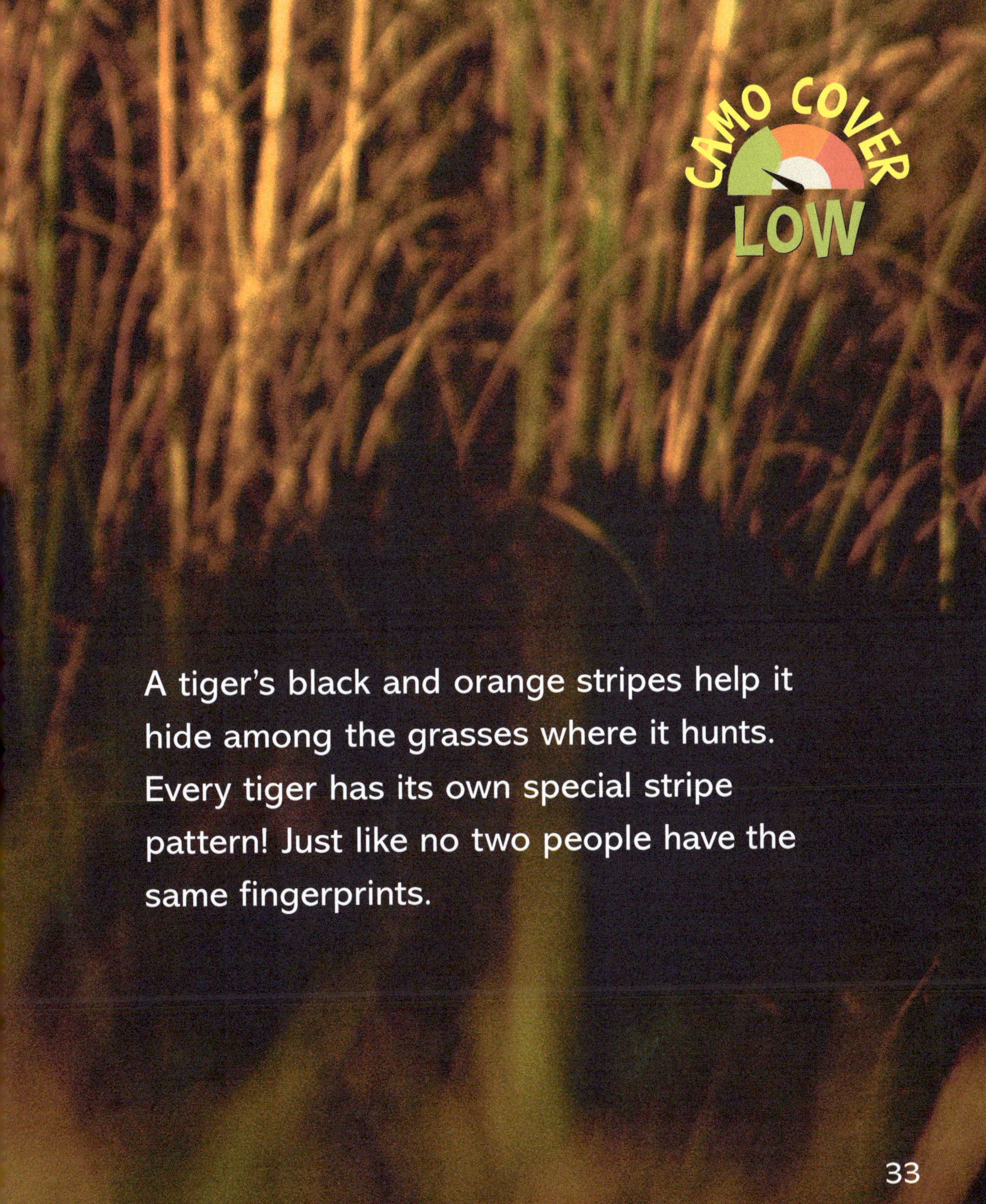

A tiger's black and orange stripes help it hide among the grasses where it hunts. Every tiger has its own special stripe pattern! Just like no two people have the same fingerprints.

ANT-MIMICKING SPIDER

Instead of matching their surroundings, some spiders pretend to be a completely different animal: an ant! Some do this to keep themselves safe from ants. Other spiders **mimic** ants so that they can get close enough to eat them!

Acrobat ant

Ant-**mimicking** spider

STICK BUG

These insects look just like what their name is: sticks and twigs. The biggest stick bug can be more than a foot (30 centimeters) long—that's almost as tall as a bowling pin! Stick bugs blend in with their **habitat** to keep them safe from **predators.**

Living Leaves

Lots of animals disguise themselves as leaves to stay hidden among trees and bushes. Look closely! Can you spot which "leaves" are animals?

Dead leaf mantis

Indian leaf butterfly

Bat-faced toad

Leaf katydid

Brick moth

MOUNTAIN HARE

This hare lives up high in the mountains. It is built for life in the cold snow! It eats the tough plants that grow on the mountainside. It burrows into snow to find shelter. And its thick, white fur helps to keep it warm and **camouflaged!**

GHOST PIPEFISH

These tiny fish are covered with beautiful details that match the corals they swim around. Pipefish float through the water without moving much, which makes it hard to tell them apart from their surroundings.

See-Through Species

Some animals hide by letting their surroundings show through their **transparent** bodies. **Transparent** means see-through.

Ghost shrimp

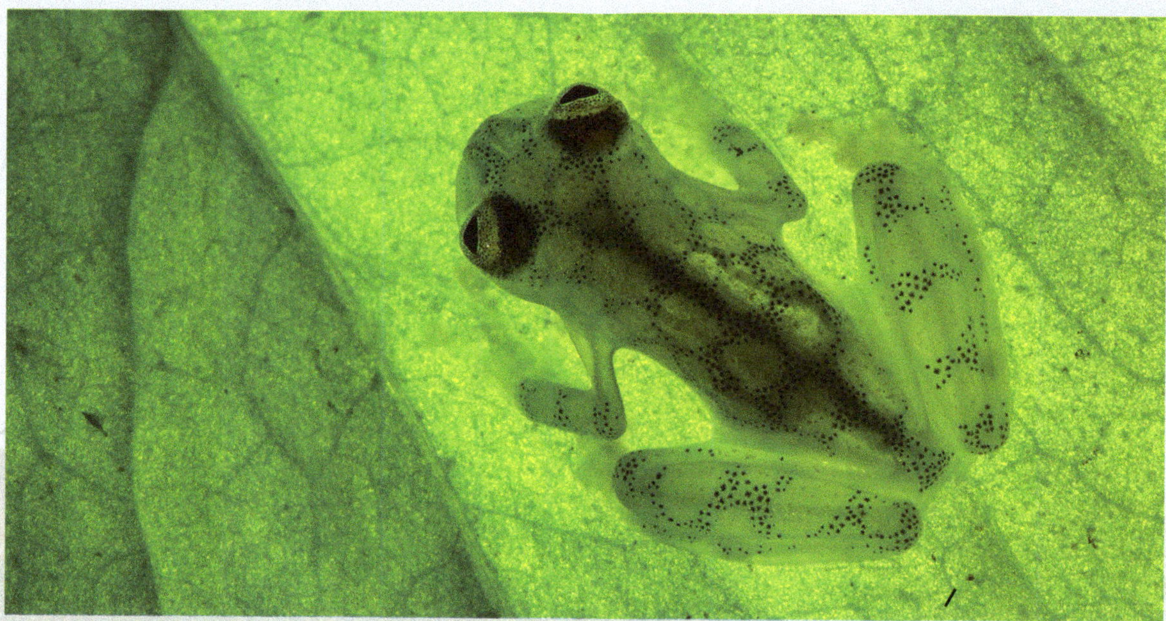

Glass frog

Glass octopus

Glasswing butterfly

Tortoiseshell beetle

Glossary

Camouflage

the natural coloring or form of an animal that lets it blend into its surroundings, making it hard to see.

Habitat

the place where a plant or animal naturally lives and grows.

Mimic

to copy the appearance of something else, such as by taking on its shape or coloring; an animal that does this.

Mimicry

the action of copying the appearance of something else, such as by taking on its shape or coloring.

Predator

an animal that hunts, kills, and eats other animals.

Prey

an animal that is hunted, killed, and eaten by another; to hunt, kill, and eat another animal.

Polyp

a simple form of a water animal, consisting largely of a stomach and a mouth with fingerlike tentacles to gather its food.

Species

a group of animals or plants that have certain traits in common and can reproduce (make more animals like themselves) with each other.

Transparent

easily seen through.

Index

A

adders, Peringuey's, 14-15
ants, acrobat, 35

B

beetles, tortoiseshell,45
birds
- grouse, wild, 10-11
- owls, snowy, 20-21

butterflies, 26
- glasswing, 45
- Indian leaf, 38
- swallowtail, 27

C

camouflage, 3
caterpillars, 26-27
chameleons, 9
colors, changing, 8-9
corals, 30-31, 42-43
cuttlefish, 8

F

fish
- flounders, 22-23
- lionfish, 17
- pipefish, ghost, 42-43
- seadragon, leafy, 18-19
- seahorses, pygmy, 30-31

foxes, Arctic, 28-29
frogs, glass, 44

G

geckos, leaf-tailed, 4-5
grouse, wild, 10-11

H

habitat, 3
hares, mountain, 40-41

I

insects
- ants, acrobat, 35
- beetles, tortoiseshell, 45
- katydids, leaf, 39
- stick bugs, 37
- *See also* butterflies; mantises; moths

K

katydids, leaf, 39

L

lionfish, 17
lizards, 4-5

M

mammals
- foxes, Arctic, 28-29
- hares, mountain, 40-41
- tigers, 32-33

mantises
- dead leaf, 38
- orchid, 6-7

moths, 26
- brick, 39
- Brussels lace, 27
- noctuid, 27
- peppered, 27

O

octopuses
- glass, 45
- mimic, 16-17

owls, snowy, 20-21

P

pipefish, ghost, 42-43

S

seadragons, leafy, 18-19
seahorses, pygmy, 30-31
shrimp, ghost, 44
snakes
- adders, Peringuey's, 14-15
- leaf-nosed twig, 12-13
- sea, 17

spiders
- ant-mimicking, 34-35
- bird-poo, 24-25
- golden crab, 9

squid, 8
stick bugs, 36-37

T

tigers, 32-33
toads, bat-faced, 39
transparent animals, 44-45

V

venom, 17

Acknowledgments

Cover: © Klein & Hubert, Nature Picture Library; © Alex Hyde, Nature Picture Library
4-5 © Nick Garbutt, Nature Picture Library; © Alex Hyde, Nature Picture Library
6-7 © Alex Hyde, Nature Picture Library; © Michael D. Kern, Nature PIcture Library
8-9 © Klein & Hubert, Nature Picture Library; © Tim Laman, Nature Picture Library; © Alex Mustard, Nature Picture Library; © Alex Hyde, Nature Picture Library
10-11 © Markus Varesvuo, Nature PIcture Library
12-13 © Nick Garbutt, Nature Picture Library; © Inaki Relanzon, Nature Picture Library
14-15 © Arno Dietz, Shutterstock; © Christophe Courteau, Nature Picture Library
16-17 © Ethan Daniels, Shutterstock; © Brandon Cole, Nature Picture Library
18-19 © Alex Mustard, Nature Picture Library
20-21 © FotoRequest/Shutterstock; © Pitipat Usanakornkul, Shutterstock
22-23 © Frei/ARCO/Nature Picture Library
24-25 © PREMAPHOTOS/Nature Picture Library
26-27 © Andrew Harrington, Nature Picture Library; © Duncan Mcewan, Nature Picture Library; © Lorraine Bennery, Nature Picture Library; © PREMAPHOTOS/Nature Picture Library; © Cyril Ruoso, Nature Picture Library
28-29 © Steven Kazlowski, Nature Picture Library; © Jenny E. Ross, Nature Picture Library
30-31 © Jurgen Freund, Nature Picture Library
32-33 © Francois Savigny, Nature Picture Library
34-35 © Tim Laman, Nature Picture Library; © Doug Wechsler, Nature Picture Library; © Stephen Dalton, Nature Picture Library
36-37 © Jan Hamrsky, Nature Picture Library
38-39 © Alessandro Bonora, Shutterstock; © Stephen Dalton, Nature Picture Library; © Adrian Davies, Nature Picture Library; © Thomas Marent, Rolfnp/Alamy Images; © Pete Oxford, Nature Picture Library; © Robert Thompson, Nature Picture Library
40-41 © Scotland: The Big Picture/Nature Picture Library
42-43 © Doug Perrine, Nature Picture Library
44-45 © Photographil8/Shutterstock; © David Shale, Nature Picture Library; © Alex Hyde, Nature Picture Library; © Solvin Zankl, Nature Picture Library; © Edwin Giesbers, Nature Picture Library; © Doug Wechsler, Nature Picture Library

www.ingramcontent.com/pod-product-compliance
Ingram Content Group UK Ltd.
Pitfield, Milton Keynes, MK11 3LW, UK
UKHW061957290726
14090UKWH00021B/1258

9 780716 650874